m

Teenage Refugees From

GUATEMALA

Speak Out

IN THEIR OWN VOICES

Teenage Refugees From

GUATEMALA

Speak Out

GERRY HADDEN

THE ROSEN PUBLISHING GROUP, INC.
NEW YORK

97 412

Published in 1997 by The Rosen Publishing Group, Inc.
29 East 21st Street, New York, NY 10010

First Edition
Copyright © 1997 by The Rosen Publishing Group, Inc.

Manufactured in the United States of America.

Library of Congress Cataloging-in-Publication Data

Teenage refugees from Guatemala speak out / [compiled by] Gerry
    Hadden. — 1st ed.
        p.   cm. — (In their own voices)
    Includes bibliographical references and index.
    Summary: Teenagers from Guatemala describe why they left that country
and how they have adjusted to life in their new homeland.
    ISBN 0-8239-2439-4
    1. Guatemalan American teenagers—Juvenile literature. 2. Refugees—
United States—Juvenile literature.   [1. Guatemalan Americans.
2. Refugees. 3. Youths' writings.] I. Hadden, Gerry. II. Series.
E184.G82T44   1997
973'.04687281—dc20   96-38916
                                                                CIP
                                                                 AC

Contents

Rigoberta Menchú Tum received the Nobel Peace Prize in 1992 for her efforts to organize the Quiché Maya people and to tell the world about their suffering. Like many other Guatemalans, she fled the country for her safety.

INTRODUCTION

Guatemala is at a crossroads. After more than thirty years of civil war, in which an estimated 200,000 people were killed, more than 1 million displaced, and a quarter million forced into neighboring Mexico and other countries, the nation's leaders have at last signed a peace accord. On December 29, 1996, rebels and the government agreed to a cease-fire on all sides. Many Guatemalans are happy, but many more are skeptical of the new peace agreement. Cease-fires have been broken many times before. Also, the new accord grants amnesty to everyone involved in the fighting, including the soldiers responsible for murdering and kidnapping thousands of Guatemalans over the last three decades. The

Nadie sabe para quien trabaja.

ENGLISH TRANSLATION FROM SPANISH:
One never knows for whom one works.

amnesty law also pardons the many rebels who committed atrocities in the name of freedom. The amnesty law angers those who want justice served for crimes committed. But in the end the two sides felt that after such a long and complicated struggle, the only way to guarantee that all sides would sign the peace treaty seemed to be by promising freedom from prosecution for everyone.

All sides in the Guatemalan conflict have one thing in common: a hope that the fighting is over once and for all, and that peace will bring stability to their impoverished country.

Since 1986 Guatemala has had a democratically elected government, but many believe that the military is in control. The fighting that began thirty years ago as a struggle for power between the army and the poor, mostly Indian, majority, continues. Most of the war's victims have been indigenous (native) Guatemalans—who make up about 65 percent of the population—and other supporters of economic and political reforms. Many Guatemalans who have tried to make reforms have been threatened or killed. Many more have left the country, fearing for their lives. Tens of thousands have fled to neighboring Mexico, Honduras, and Belize. Some of these refugees, with the help of the United Nations, have begun to return to Guatemala, but they face many obstacles.

Guatemala's current problems began in 1944. A new democratic government led by Juan José Arévalo tried to take back power from the foreign companies and governments that had been taking advantage of the country for years. Arévalo introduced reforms to make life better for farmers and laborers. However, by 1954 the U.S. government had grown suspicious of communist influence in the new government. The United States feared a communist takeover within the northern hemisphere. In order to protect the interests of the large American companies, the U.S. government helped overthrow the Guatemalan government. With support from the U.S. Central Intelligence Agency, a new dictatorship was established. The new dictatorship soon began a campaign to make supporters of the democratic movement "disappear." Government troops and unofficial death squads murdered many people in the name of halting what they called a "communist revolution." But guerrillas, or anti-government rebels, resisted fiercely. The two sides have been fighting ever since. They continued their armed struggle until the signing of the peace accord in December 1996.

In order to understand the roots of the problems in modern Guatemala, one must examine the violence that erupted between the first Spanish explorers and Native Guatemalans more than 450 years ago. Before the Europeans came in 1524, the largest native group in Guatemala, the Mayans, had a complex, flourishing society. It was based on agriculture and was not dependent on outside forces or international economies.

When the Spanish arrived, they took over much of the Mayan people's lands and forced them to work without pay. Mayan slavery made a few landowners extremely rich. For the Mayan civilization, the results were disastrous. As the Spanish settlers, or *criollos*, became wealthy, native communities were destroyed. A class system emerged that was based on a sense of Spanish ethnic superiority. Millions of indigenous people were killed or enslaved by the forces of racism and greed.

Today, Guatemala shares many of the same problems as other developing nations. Malnutrition, unknown 500 years ago, persists throughout the country. More than 85 percent of the population lives in poverty. Most land is still owned by a small group of very wealthy people, some from other countries. The political climate can be dangerous for anyone who opposes the government.

The plight of the Guatemalan people gained international recognition in 1992 when Rigoberta Menchú Tum, a Quiché Maya woman, received the Nobel Peace Prize for her efforts to organize her people against the genocide occurring in the country.

The people of Guatemala have survived severe military abuse, economic exploitation, and political instability. With their recently elected government, citizens hope the fighting will end. But after so many years of civil war, the people are also wary—and with good reason. In October 1995, several refugees returning to their village after many years of exile in Mexico were massacred by government troops. The Guatemalan government and the United Nations have investigated the incident, but to date nothing has come of it. That massacre, like so many others, may be officially forgotten under the terms of the peace accord. Guatemala now moves ahead on a shaky ground of peace. Until some level of prosperity comes to the country, young Guatemalans will most likely continue to make their way to the United States in search of a better life.◆

Thomas comes from a Mayan village in the mountains of Guatemala. His father and brothers were killed by the Guatemalan army when they tried to reclaim the land that had been stolen from them. Thomas has struggled to overcome this shattering experience and rebuild his life.

THOMAS
WE LOST EVERYTHING

My name is Thomas. I'm eighteen years old. I live in Vancouver, British Columbia, Canada. I came to Canada from Los Angeles when I was thirteen. I came to the United States by myself. I was able to cross the border from Mexico to Texas. I was working in Brownsville, Texas. One day I just decided to stay in the United States. Then I made my way across Texas to Los Angeles. I came to Vancouver by bus.

When I arrived in the United States I didn't know anyone. I lived in a shelter. It was my first time outside Guatemala.

I originally come from a small town near Quezaltenango. It's called Totoniqapan. It's a village in the mountains. About twenty families live there, or about 200 people. Our people grow crops, mainly corn. We are Mayans. We speak Quiché, not Spanish, though I also speak Spanish. I learned Spanish from Mexican people in Los Angeles.

I spent three years in Los Angeles. I've been in Vancouver for one year. I came here from Los Angeles because I was working for two dollars an hour, and it wasn't enough. I worked in a factory making clothes. The work wasn't so hard, but I worked long hours for little pay. The factory was illegal.

I have to send money to my mother in Guatemala. She's living in Guatemala City now because we had to leave our village. Some people came and took our land.

The army came with these people who tried to say that our land was theirs, and that it had belonged to their ancestors. They already had money and land elsewhere. But they wanted our land for farming. They talked to our people through translators since we didn't speak Spanish. We got our own translators, but the rich people paid them to translate the papers differently so we'd give away our land. We trusted the translators and lost everything.

My dad and my two older brothers were killed by these people. One day my dad and my brothers returned to the village to demand our land back. They never came home. The government wouldn't help us find out what happened.

That made me the oldest kid in the family. We moved to Guatemala City. We changed our names. My other two brothers and little sister are still there. This happened five years ago. Here in the United States, I changed my name again.

My mother is working in Guatemala City, selling clothes on the street.

My old plan was to buy different land in Guatemala and forget everything that happened. But now I realize that it's more difficult than that. I've gone twice to Alaska to work in the fishing industry because you can make good money doing that. I went once in the summer, and once from January to April. I was on a boat. It was hard. I worked eighteen hours a day. If you don't speak English they treat you badly. If you try to say that you don't want to work, then they kick you off the boat, and you can never work for them again. I sent most of the money to my mom. It went a long way in Guatemala.

I've changed my plan now, though. I want to bring my family here. But it's not legally possible.

I like Vancouver. I discovered that if you study something, it can help your future. In L.A. I was only speaking Spanish, so I didn't know how much I had to learn. In L.A. I got a fake ID—fake everything—so that I could work. That's why I can't give you a photo. My old employers might know that I'm illegal.

Recently, I spoke at a high school in Washington. There were kids from many different

These Quiché Maya girls wear the colorful woven clothing that is typical of their region. Each Maya region uses unique patterns and colors in its clothing design.

countries. We each spoke for ten minutes about what life is like in our countries. There were 600 ninth-graders in the audience. I was scared! They didn't ask questions. They only sat and listened while we talked. We went to speak at that school because it's in the countryside, and the kids don't know a lot about how the United States is made up of people from all different countries. Everyone in the audience was white, except for four or five people.

In Guatemala I didn't go to school too much. When I first came here I saw about 20,000 books in the library. It was so different because we didn't have any books in my home. My parents didn't go to high school. I only had three years of school. I could read only a little bit of Spanish. My language, Quiché, is only a spoken language, not a written language.

I speak to my family occasionally. Because they don't have a phone at home, they go to a public phone at a certain time, and I call them. But it's expensive.

I've made some older friends who are medical students here in the university. Now they're doctors doing their residencies. I am maturing because I'm learning about life and about different things. I like school a lot. When I went to L.A. I started to read everything I could in Spanish about religion, politics, and other subjects. Now I'm doing the same with English.

I would like to study political science or maybe medicine. My dream is to return to the mountains in Guatemala to show my people how to do something different, like how to read. Maybe I'll teach Spanish. My people are very intelligent. They've discovered that the Mayans knew how to do brain and heart surgery hundreds of years ago. This knowledge is lost now, but once they could do it. We have a lot of potential, but we can't show it because of the problems in Guatemala. It's so hard there because of the years of war. One hundred and fifty thousand people have been killed. One hundred thousand children lost at least one of their parents. Most of the victims are Indians. There are no schools in Indian villages now.

The Guatemalan government calls us communists. The United States sends millions to support the Guatemalan army in this fight, and the army supports the rich people. Most of the people fighting are Mayans, because they lost their families. But before my father and brothers were killed, our family didn't care about guerrillas or fighting.

The guerrillas came and told my family about things happening in other towns and villages, but we didn't care about this. We tried to keep ourselves separate from it. The guerrillas wanted us to join the fight. They said one day the army would come to our town. They were right.

The Guatemalan government doesn't want us to have schools because, if we become educated, then we can cause problems for them. The recent elections were fake. I have no faith in our political system. It only helps the rich people. The army controls everything. Most of the people are fighting over food, not over ideas. They just want to grow food and get an education.

Sometimes it makes me laugh that in the United States and Canada a bus takes you from your home to school! In Guatemala sometimes you have to walk very far to get to school. You have to bring your own chair if you want one, and your own chalkboard.

Right now I'm most interested in learning. I'm not very good at playing most sports, like basketball. I didn't have the opportunity to play those things at home. I started working when I was seven years old.

I stay at school from 8:00 AM to 4:00 PM, and then I go to a center to learn more English. Every time I go there I learn something new. Sometimes just one or two words, but that's why I go. When you know something, it's yours for life. It can help you.

I don't watch television. I spend my free time in the library, looking at books or doing homework.

I've learned how to make opportunities for myself here. When I first arrived, I tried hard to learn English. I went to the library, but I couldn't find anything. But six months ago, somebody told me about some ESL classes. I went there, and they helped me. In L.A. I tried to go to school, but they asked for my Social Security number, and I didn't have one. This school didn't ask me. All they wanted was my birth certificate, which I have. This school gives you an idea about what high school here is like. It helped me be prepared.

I live here with a friend from Guatemala. He's twenty-five, and we can speak Quiché together. We met at the shelter. There's a whole group of Guatemalans here.

Canadian students are very nice, but some don't have a lot of responsibilities. They have everything already. It's been hard to make friends, but I also haven't tried too hard, mostly because I'm still in ESL classes. Sometimes Canadians don't

In 1993, efforts began to return Guatemalan refugees to Guatemala from Mexico. These were among the sixty-five buses that carried more than 2,000 refugees back to Guatemala.

want to talk to me because my English isn't great. I think they get bored.

Sometimes I work as a landscaper. I go to a local shelter early in the morning on weekends and wait for the trucks to come by. Many Latinos are there waiting for work, too. It's pretty crazy. Everyone runs for the trucks. The strong survive. Every Saturday and Sunday I do this. Sometimes I have to push other people out of the way, but I always get work.

I did restaurant work, but it's hard. In one restaurant, they didn't pay me my money. I worked on Christmas, and I kept calling for my check, but they wouldn't give it to me. That's why I hate restaurant work. They take advantage of you, especially if you're illegal.

I worked for a coffee shop for a little while. They had photographs of little children in my country drinking coffee in their indigenous clothes. I think they have to do this to be able to sell their coffee. And those people, my people, can't see the reality. They have nothing—they have no perspective on the world because they are so poor. They're only working. When the coffee company people go to Guatemala, the army takes them to only the beautiful places. They don't go to the mountains or to the *fincas* (coffee plantations). They don't know how many children are dying from picking coffee. The photos aren't real.

Sometimes it hurts that I don't really have freedom here. And I don't have it at home, either. It's not easy because when you have to work, you don't have time for anything else. I would like to be like the other kids who have their parents, their families, and enough food.

Now I live in an apartment. My first three months I lived on the street. I think that as long as I don't do anything bad it will be OK. I'm just trying to understand everything. That way, I can take responsibility for my own life, not blame someone else. I'm not afraid of being caught here, but I am afraid for my family if I can't send them money.

I have a friend who wants to support me if I make it to college. She's Canadian. I met her because when I was at the shelter, I needed to go to an eye doctor. She was the doctor. We talked a lot and became friends. I showed her that I didn't need her money or support, that I could support myself. She respected that. She told me that she'd send me money if I go home to go to college. But it's hard to study at the university in Guatemala because most of the guerrillas come from there. It's a hundred times more dangerous to be there. Most of the young people who disappeared were at the university. In one week, forty young people disappeared.

I don't think I have the courage to live in Guatemala. If I did, I wouldn't be here. When I think that there are young girls in the mountains fighting for my people, and I'm here in Canada, I feel ashamed. They are being tortured and are killed—just for teaching people how to read! Meanwhile, I'm here, not doing anything. Sometimes I believe that I am a coward.◆

Iliana and her parents came to the United States because her uncle was killed. Her brother and sister still live in Guatemala, and she hopes that her family will be reunited someday.

ILIANA
BELIEF IN GOD

My name is Iliana. I come from the city of Quezaltenango. I'm thirteen years old. I've been here eight months.

Quezaltenango doesn't have huge buildings like Seattle, but there are a lot of people and a lot of noise. I miss the noise. We listen for it here sometimes. At home we could always hear the traffic, the street workers, all the people.

We're *ladinos*. We have a little Mayan blood in our family. Just about every family in Guatemala does, though a "Mayan" race doesn't really exist anymore. There are now twenty-three separate Indian nations, each one different. But though each has a different language, there are many similarities. Customs are also similar.

My mom was a psychologist in Guatemala. She worked with kids. Here she works for a women's cooperative supporting Latino women. My father was a lawyer and worked for an organization trying to improve the lives of poor people.

We left because my uncle was killed in the office where he worked. He was an important businessman in Guatemala. The police said it was suicide, but we don't believe them. After that, my parents found out that the government was listening to our phone calls. So they decided we should leave. I came to the United States in a plane with my father. We flew through Miami, then through Dallas. We came here to Seattle because my other uncle lives here. My dad had visited the United States four times before we moved, and my mom had visited once.

My older sister is still in Guatemala, in Guatemala City. She's at the university there. She's an artist. She's involved in some social causes, so she has to watch out for herself, like we did. My brother still lives in our house in Quezaltenango. He was very afraid because strange things have happened since the death of our uncle.

My brother and sister couldn't leave with us. My parents and I could get visas, but my brother is close to eighteen years old. Since he is almost an adult, he couldn't come with my parents. My sister is older than my brother, so she wasn't allowed. Now we're trying to think of a way to get my

Many refugees from the civil war in Guatemala fled to the neighboring state of Chiapas, Mexico. These Guatemalan refugee children study in a refugee camp in Chiapas in 1992.

brother here. After all, he is living alone, and our sister is all the way in Guatemala City. He talks with her, of course, but he feels lonely without Mom, Dad, and me.

I study the usual things in school. I like art and math and health the most. I also like English. It's interesting. I've always told my dad that I want to become a nun when I grow up. I believe very strongly in God. We're Catholic. We go to a Catholic church here. It's just like home. I want to study art at the university, too.

The kids here are different in many ways from kids in Guatemala. They're basically the same, but they have different customs. For example, here we eat lunch in school; in Guatemala we always walked home for lunch. Many of the classes are also different.

In Guatemala, I played basketball with my cousins after school. We also played with dolls. I have one cousin, Monica, who is my best friend. We are very close. We're the same age. We were always together. Now we write to each other, but we haven't spoken since I moved here.

When I first got here I was going to a different school than the school I'm in now. The students there were a little different than here in Seattle. They said that I was different just because I came from a foreign country, and because the color of my skin is darker. I've seen a little bit of racism here, but not much. I've made some American friends. Some kids think that if you're Latino you must be from Mexico. I have to tell them that I'm from Guatemala, in Central America.

I'd like to return to Guatemala because all my cousins and family are there. I like the United States, but I'd rather go back. I wasn't really afraid before we left, but we had to leave. There was crime in Guatemala, like here, but you learn how to protect yourself. Here it's even more difficult because you don't know your neighbors. There seem to be more crazy people here, maybe because everyone is so individualistic. Also, drugs are more common here.

Another thing that makes me feel strange here is that some people have a sense of superiority over others. I think everyone's the same, but some people don't believe this. It's true that this attitude exists in every country, including Guatemala, but here it's stronger.

The weather here is very different, too. In Guatemala it's either hot or cold, depending on where you live. It doesn't change. Quezaltenango is in the mountains, at an altitude of 2,500 meters, so it's always cold. But it doesn't snow in my country.

I watch television for fun. I also draw pictures. I draw pictures of my thoughts, and how I feel. It's like a diary, but when something happens, I draw about it instead of writing about it.

I don't know what's going to happen in my country. The politicians say that things are going to change, but in reality they don't. I don't think things will ever change. If I could have one wish, I would bring the rest of my family here. Then I'd be happier.◆

Sandra, a successful athlete, lives in Connecticut. She hopes to be a hairstylist someday.

SANDRA
WE'RE NOT AFRAID

I'm seventeen years old, and a senior in high school. I come from Guatemala City. I first came to the United States with my grandmother. My parents were already here. They came here when I was one year old. From age one to age seven I lived with my grandmother in Guatemala. Then she brought me here. I lived in the South Bronx (a section of New York City) for a year. Then my family moved to Connecticut.

My father was the first to come here, hoping to find work. My mother followed later. Right now my father works in a factory where they make pots. He's been there for fifteen years. In Guatemala he did odd jobs, but the pay wasn't good.

This Guatemalan refugee girl cares for her younger brother and sister in a refugee camp. Thousands of children became orphans during the civil war.

When my father got here he stopped writing to my mom. So she came looking for him since she didn't have any money. She found him somehow, and they're still together. She's a housecleaner here. In Guatemala she didn't work outside the home.

I have a younger brother who is fifteen. I have some other family members here—an uncle and three cousins. I have relatives in California and Chicago, too. I still have lots of family in Guatemala.

I play soccer for my high school, and this year I'll play basketball for the junior varsity team.

I like hairstyling a lot, so I'll probably get a license for that. Then I want to study business and open my own salon.

The first time I visited Guatemala three years ago, I felt like everything had changed. It's worse now. The pollution is worse and it's crowded. I like to visit, but I don't want to live there. I speak Spanish mostly at home, but English with my friends. I don't feel American; it's just that I'm used to things here and have more advantages here.

My friends here are all different. Some are Latinos; some are Americans. Everything's mixed. My American friends are curious about Guatemala. I tell them it's like any other country. There are nice places, and there are poor places.

Next year I'll become an American citizen. My mother already is one.

Tikal National Park in northern Guatemala is home to majestic Mayan pyramids and temples. Tikal is one of Guatemala's main tourist attractions.

Some people don't understand why we're here. They say we should go back. But it's just ignorance. Everyone has problems. You can't just say, "Go back to your country." It's complicated. Many people don't make enough money to live in Guatemala. They might have a family to support. Last year, a girl in school wrote a paper on illegal immigrants, saying they cause problems. I felt she shouldn't say that. I asked her, "What's the difference if I come from a Spanish-speaking country? Your family came from another country once, too."

There will always be racism. There are some

really nice people and some really stupid people.

Some people who come from a different country work hard, but not all of them. Most study to get ahead because they know how hard life can be. Sometimes it seems like American kids take what they have for granted.

We're not afraid of the government or the fighting. My father wants to buy a house in Guatemala. He wants to move back. He visited and saw his old friends. He relived old memories. But I felt uncomfortable because I wasn't used to it. I have some memories, but now I'd be scared to walk the streets by myself. I'm used to a quieter place.◆

Alfonzo lives in Seattle, Washington. He finds it difficult to be separated from his father, but enjoys his hobbies and his friends of many nationalities.

ALFONZO
LIFE HERE IS EASIER

My name is Alfonzo. I'm from the city of Reu in Guatemala. I am part Indian and part Latin. I came to the United States two years ago. My mother and my twenty-year-old sister came three years ago because we were having big problems with money. My mom had her own restaurant. I'm not sure what happened, but she had to sell it because it failed. After she sold it, she said, "Well, I am going to go to the United States." So for a year before I came here I lived with my father in Guatemala.

My parents were divorced when I was ten. My father moved to another house, and that's when my mom started the restaurant. My father is a truck driver. He has no plans to live in the United

States. He was in California. He lived in the United States to buy trucks for his business, then went back to Guatemala.

I'm here illegally, so I can't work. But I'm not afraid of being caught. If they send me back to Guatemala, that will be OK. I like it here, but it's very different. Everything is so big—the houses, the freeways. I miss my home, my friends, and the weather in Guatemala.

My town, Reu, is on the coast. Reu is known for its clothing and coffee. They also grow sugarcane. The beaches there are nice. My grandma lives in the countryside, and I used to visit her a lot. It was only twenty-six miles away from Reu.

When I left, I was in my first year of high school. School is different in Guatemala. For one thing, you study six years to get the basic diploma. Then, you study three more years, and go to a university. I like school here better. They give you food and books. Everything is free. In Reu you have to buy everything—books, pens, paper, and food.

My mom wants to move back to Guatemala next December, but I don't want to go back with her. I've made lots of friends here. My friends are Filipinos, other Latinos, and one Laotian. I don't have too many American friends. It's not that it's hard to make American friends, but they're different than we are. They don't like the same things. For instance, I like Latin music and rap, but most Americans like their rock. Also, our food is

A group of Kaibiles, special forces within the Guatemalan army, marches in formation in 1989. The Kaibiles have been blamed for incidents of torture and violence in Guatemalan villages.

different. But I still want to stay because I want to finish high school here. I can't go to college here, though, because I'm illegal.

One of my favorite things to do is play chess. I'm not very good, but I love it. I also play football—not on the team, though, because I'm too young. Sometimes I play soccer with friends, too.

My seventeen-year-old sister came with me to the United States two years ago. She has a baby daughter whom I take care of after school because my sister works in a bakery. My sister pays me ten dollars a day to baby-sit. When we came here she was pregnant. She and the father had split up, so he didn't come. My oldest sister works in a restaurant with my mom. She wants to go back to Guatemala and buy some land and build a house. My other sister—the one with the child—doesn't want to go back.

When I'm finished with school I'm going to be a police officer somewhere. It's fun work, and I want to help people.

We came to the United States with the help of some people you can pay to take you across the border. My mom paid a woman, and she arranged it. It took us twenty-two days. First we crossed the Mexican border in a car. It can be a problem, but we paid some people to help us. From there we took a boat traveling to Tijuana. It's a city close to the California border. We just walked across the border from Tijuana into the United States. The first time we tried, the border police caught us and threw us in jail. We were there for six hours. It wasn't too scary. The police were nice, except for one American woman who was very mad at us. They asked us where we were from, and we said Mexico so that they wouldn't send us all the way back to Guatemala. They only sent us back to Tijuana.

One morning around 4:00 AM we tried again. This time we made it. It was very cold. We climbed a big hill and hid near a street. We stayed there until a man came. He was expecting us. We went into a tunnel for twenty minutes. Eventually we saw a light. When we came out, a truck was

In 1991, Guatemalan soldiers search passengers on a public bus traveling through the Petén jungle. The military had set up a checkpoint in the area because the guerrillas had a strong presence there.

waiting for us and we drove to Los Angeles. In L.A. I saw a friend of mine from El Salvador and two guys from my town. They saw me and said, "Oh, Alfonzo! How are you?"

We stayed in L.A. two days, and then they brought us here to Seattle. We came because my mom was here. She came because she had a friend who told her that life is easier in Seattle. And it is. Some people here, at the church, give you food. In California they don't do that.

There are many languages in Guatemala. They teach Spanish in school. The Mayan language, Quiché, is very hard to learn.

When I first arrived in the United States, I went to a school for ESL (English as a Second Language). The only English I knew was the colors, how to count to ten, and "I am." That's all! I had a great teacher, but he died last year. Now I'm in a regular high school. I like English a lot, but I like Spanish more. I also like science and math.

I haven't talked to my dad since I left. I miss him a lot. He lived about twenty miles from me. Right before I left, I told him that I wanted to see him next week. The next day I went to a friend's house, and she told me not to go home because my father was going to try to take me away to live with him. We drove by my house together, and it was true. He was there waiting for me. He didn't want me to live with my mother. He didn't catch me, though. My sister has his address, but she won't give it to me. She's written him three letters and sent him some money, but he hasn't written back.

In Guatemala the fighting between the government and the guerrillas is still happening, but my family isn't involved. The guerrillas are mostly Indians. One night there was fighting down the street from my house. The army came in helicopters to catch the guerrillas, but they got away. They escaped in the dark.

Sometimes the guerrillas blow up bridges. I don't like when this happens because you have to wait a long time if you want to visit another town. They build a new, smaller bridge, and it just gets blown up again.

I want to talk to my friends in Guatemala. It's been two years now since we spoke. I miss them a lot. If I had their addresses I would write to them, but I don't. I hope that one day I will see them again.◆

Ligia has lived in the United States for ten years, but she has returned to Guatemala several times to visit relatives. She often feels a conflict between the Guatemalan and American aspects of her upbringing.

LIGIA
CAUGHT IN BETWEEN

My name is Ligia. I'm fifteen years old. I was born in Guatemala City. My family lived just ten minutes outside the city. Now I live in Stamford, Connecticut.

Guatemala City is very crowded. I really don't like some parts of the city. There are too many people, and the streets are dirty. But there are some nice parts. It's just not my style of living.

I came to the United States ten years ago, when I was six years old. I came with my mom and my two sisters. My dad came about six months later.

In Guatemala, my mom was a military nurse and worked in a military hospital. My dad was an electrician. We left because my parents needed to

The National Palace is located in the capital, Guatemala City.

earn more money. Their plan was to come to the United States, earn more, and then go back. We've stayed longer than expected. Because of the political situation in Guatemala, we didn't have to leave the United States.

We're middle class here. My mom is a house-cleaner. It's easier for my parents because my sisters don't live with us anymore. I have two sisters; one lives in Queens, New York, and one just got married. I'm the youngest.

I go back to Guatemala every summer and stay with my aunt or my grandmother outside Guatemala City for vacation. We go out to different places, like to the river to swim. I don't have any friends in Guatemala because I left when I was so young. But I have a bunch of cousins who I hang out with. My family is pretty big, especially on my dad's side.

The first time I went back, I didn't remember my aunt. I knew who she was, but I didn't recognize her face or the faces of others from my past. I remember having fun in school playing with the other kids during recess, but I didn't stay in touch with them when we left.

I want to go back to Guatemala. My friends here look at me like I'm crazy but I have more fun over there. I think it's because when I'm there I'm with my own family, and my parents let me do more things because I'm with relatives.

I feel caught in between cultures even though I came to the United States at an early age. It's because my parents have raised me as a Guatemalan. Over there you can't go out as much and you can't talk on the phone as much. Here kids can stay out really late. But I can't even sleep over at people's houses, because that's just not how we do it. So I feel like a Guatemalan, but I also feel like an American. Sometimes it's frustrating. Sometimes I really like being in Guatemala, but then I miss being here. I want to be in both places at the same time!

My Spanish is nearly perfect, so I won't have a language problem when I return. If I go back I'll probably take three years of courses in tourism. I am also thinking of becoming a civil engineer.

I'm on the swim team at school. Right now I'm looking for a job and studying. My parents don't want me to get a job, but this summer, before I move back permanently, my mom said I can work.

I watch the news every day here, but I'm not into the politics of Guatemala. I don't really talk to my parents about our government, but sometimes I overhear them talking about it and catch things they say. My family is not really afraid to go back. My mom sometimes thinks about how poor the people are, and how because of that the people have to steal. It's not very safe sometimes, and that concerns her. But she really misses it, so she's going back.

Most American teenagers don't know anything about Guatemala. Before, when people used to ask me where I'm from, I'd say "Guatemala," and they would have no clue where that was. I'd say, "How could you not know?" One of my friends thought it was an island somewhere!

Americans should understand that there is a mix of different people in Guatemala, just like in the United States. The people there are poor, but they want to succeed, like Americans. We're just like everybody else: intelligent, wanting to succeed. It's just that the situation is so bad over there that many people just want to get out of the country.

When I first arrived, I didn't really make too many friends because we moved around a lot. I used to live in Queens (a borough of New York City). We've been in Stamford for a couple of years, so I have made some good friends here. Before, none of my friends were Hispanic, but then I met some other Hispanics. One of my best friends is from the Philippines. We talk a lot and realize that our countries are very similar. We have fun remembering and comparing.

Of all my friends, it seems like everybody who goes back to his or her country to visit doesn't want to leave. Everybody here seems like they're only interested in making money and not in other things. For example, here in Stamford, there's nothing to do. It gets kind of boring. That's why it's a relief to go back. In Guatemala my cousins and I go to different parts of the country with my uncle, who travels for business. The whole family goes on trips. It's so much fun.

I'll miss my friends a lot when I leave. I feel like they're my family, since I don't have a lot of family here. I'm only a resident here, so I'll have to get a permit to go to Guatemala without losing my residency. But it means I have to come back to the States. I don't want to lose my residency, in case I don't like Guatemala. I wanted to be a U.S. citizen before I leave, but it seems unlikely. If I stay here until I'm eighteen, my mom is afraid I won't want to go back. I could have a good future here because of my grades and everything. I'm an honor student.

In 1993, demonstrators hold newspapers proclaiming the fall from power of President Jorge Serrano Elías. Serrano was ousted from office by the Guatemalan army. Since 1945, Guatemala has suffered from unstable governments and periods of civil war.

I'm not sure if I'll come back to the United States. I'm going to give Guatemala a try, but if the situation is too difficult, and I can't get a really good job, I think I'd return to the United States. I wouldn't want to, but I'd have to.◆

Hamilton feels that he has adopted an American attitude as he focuses on his future. He plans a career in business.

HAMILTON
NOW I THINK LIKE AMERICANS

I'm sixteen and a junior in high school. I'm from Quezaltenango, the second biggest city in Guatemala. But I lived in Guatemala City for three years before coming here. I've been in the United States for four years. I came here with my sister. She's eleven now, and was seven when we came. We flew to El Paso to get our immigration papers.

My mom was already living in New Jersey. She wanted us to come join her. She came in 1984. She was a teacher, and in Guatemala they don't get paid very much. So she came to the United States to earn a better living to take care of us. She taught in an elementary school. She's a nanny now and has been with the same family for eleven years. It's like she's a part of their family. We live with my uncle here. He owns a cleaning company.

I haven't been back to visit Guatemala since I came here. I lived in Guatemala with my grandmother after my mom came to the United States. My father passed away when I was one year old. I don't remember him. He was a doctor. While on his motorcycle, my father was hit by a drunk driver. My mother didn't know what to do to take care of us.

I play soccer, which is Guatemala's main sport. I'm also in the Spanish Club. Last year I was in the International Club.

I like the United States, but it is different. In Guatemala you can go out and play with your friends. Here everything moves faster. You go to school, study, watch television, and play sports. Also, the weather here changes a lot. During the winter you can't really go out. In Guatemala, in my city, the climate is always the same. You can play all year round. I lived outside the city in a valley. We'd go to the city on our bikes or on foot. I hardly ever went to the city, though; I stayed near my house. I miss Guatemala a lot, especially when I can't go out much.

I have a lot of Latino friends but also a lot of American friends, blacks and whites.

Here kids are thinking about college. At home we didn't think about the future so much. We just lived day by day, taking things as they came. Now

I think like Americans. I want to go to college. I want to study business administration. I want to learn more about how my family business runs. I've seen how it works and I want to have my own.

I'm not sure if I want to return to Guatemala. Maybe when I'm older and have had my own business for some time. Then when I'm retired, I'll go back.

Some kids I've met here know where Guatemala is; some don't. My close friends ask me what it's like, and what sports we play.

Here, the schools want you to go to college. At home, no one pushes you. I don't go out too much here, even though friends invite me. I'm trying to take care of my schoolwork, so I can do well. I only go out on weekends.

Sometimes it can be hard to make friends. You really have to adapt yourself. Some people come here from other countries and just stick with their own kind and don't try to meet new people. If you want to be successful, you have to adapt to your surroundings; otherwise you're just like a visitor. I'm still Guatemalan, but I act American because this is where I live. If I went home I'd be Guatemalan again.◆

Henry plans to join the Air Force when he finishes school. After his father left his family, his mother worked very hard to make a life for her children in Guatemala and the United States.

HENRY
I'M NOT GOING BACK

My name is Henry. I'm fifteen years old. I'm a Guatemalan and an American. I lived in Guatemala during my early childhood. I came to the United States and started first grade in San Francisco. I speak English and Spanish.

My mom came up here for a better life and a better job. She has four other kids. She wanted the best for us. They weren't paying her that much in Guatemala. She worked on a farm picking coffee. My aunt came here first, probably eighteen years ago. Then my uncle came. He eventually brought my mom. When she came to the United States she was already pregnant with me. My dad took me back to Guatemala after I was born, and when we moved to the United States some years later, all my brothers and sisters came with us. But then my dad took off. I haven't seen him since I was six years old. I don't know if my mom has heard from him or not.

My dad owned a little shopping mall in Guatemala City. It was pretty polluted there. All the streets were dirty. But there were some places that were really nice. My uncle lived in a two-story house and had a nice car, which down there means you're rich. There are two kinds of people, rich and poor.

It was hard for us growing up because my mom was always working. She washed dishes in a restaurant in San Francisco. Then she got a job as a chef. Now she cooks in an Italian restaurant.

I moved about six months ago because I was having some gang problems and couldn't go to school. I didn't think I was in any trouble, but my mom did. She decided I should live with my uncle.

I feel both American and Guatemalan. I'm a *ladino*, which means I have Indian blood and Spanish blood. The Indian comes from my mom's side of the family. I don't really know about my dad's side.

I feel different from Americans because physically I'm much darker. Most Americans are blond and white-skinned. I was also raised in a Guatemalan-style family, with lots of relatives around me.

I went back to Guatemala two years ago for a month. I went to Tikal to see the pyramids. My family is from the village Los Seresos. My grandpa still lives there. He is just relaxing at home. I visited him while I was there. All my aunts and uncles and cousins are in San Francisco.

I don't want to move back to Guatemala because you can't get paid a lot for work. Even the best jobs pay nothing compared to here. A dollar here is like five dollars there.

No one here ever asks me what Guatemala's like. I have friends who are both Latino and American. My girlfriend here is American.

I'm a freshman in high school because I messed up last year. When I get out of school I want to join the Air Force. I played football this year for my high school. I also play basketball. I'm an average student in school. My favorite subject is math; I get A's in it. My least favorite subject is world history.

People take our culture really seriously in my country, so it's nice to go visit there and see everything. Our educational system is more advanced in Guatemala. We learn algebra in sixth grade. But the universities are better here. I'm not going back.◆

Glossary

communist A person who supports communism, a system in which property is owned by the state and is shared by everyone.

criollos Spanish settlers in Guatemala.

democratic election An election in which all eligible citizens of a country vote to elect governmental representatives.

dictatorship A country ruled by a dictator—a person who rules with complete authority.

exile To make a person leave his or her home or country, often as punishment.

genocide The deliberate destruction of an ethnic, cultural, or political group.

guerrilla A fighter who is not a member of a regular army and attacks the enemy in sudden raids.

hemisphere The northern half or the southern half of the earth, divided by the equator.

impoverished Living in extreme poverty.

indigenous Native to a country or region.

ladino Of Indian and Spanish descent.

Latino A person born or living in Latin America.

malnutrition A physical condition due to poor nourishment or lack of adequate food and nutrients.

Maya A group of Indian peoples chiefly in Guatemala, Belize, and Yucatán who speak the Mayan language (Quiché).

oppression Cruel or unjust treatment, to keep people from bettering themselves or to deny them freedom.

For Further Reading

Cummins, Ronnie. *Guatemala*. Milwaukee, WI:
   Gareth Stevens Inc., 1990.
Lazo, Carolina. *Rigoberta Menchú*. Columbus, OH:
   Silver Burdett Press, 1994.
Murphy, Gene, Ph.D. *Maya*. Danbury, CT: Grolier
   Educational Corporation, 1995.

Challenging Reading
Carmack, Robert M., ed. *Harvest of Violence: The
   Maya Indians and the Guatemalan Crisis.*
   Norman, OK: University of Oklahoma Press,
   1988.
Perera, Victor. *Unfinished Conquest: The
   Guatemalan Tragedy*. Berkeley: University of
   California Press, 1993.

Index

About the Author

Gerry Hadden is a writer and musician who lives in Seattle, Washington. He is the author of *Teenage Refugees From Mexico Speak Out* and co-author of *Home Tree Home* (Penguin). He is also a reporter and news anchor for KPLU, a National Public Radio station.

Photo Credits

Cover and pp. 6, 16, 34, Anako Editions; pp. 24, 36, 46, 50, 52, AP/Wide World Photos; p. 39, Kathleen Foster/Impact Visuals; pp. 41, 56, David Maung/Impact Visuals; pp. 20, 44, Paul Dix/Impact Visuals; pp. 12, 27, Piet van Lier/Impact Visuals; p. 30, Orlando Martin/Impact Visuals; p. 32, Marilyn Anderson/Impact Visuals.

Layout and Design

Kim Sonsky